MY BOOKS RECOMMENDATIONS

Huzaifa Surti

My Book Recommendations

My Book Recommendations

Copyright

Copyright © 2020 by Huzaifa Surti

Author Bio

Huzaifa Surti is a Youtuber, Speaker, Writer blogger, and author of two books

Huzaifa is an influencer with a positive mindset. He believes in the power of positive thinking and writes about inspiring people not to give up on their dreams and become their greatest version.

He writes extensively on success, self-development, productivity, and motivation. his writing is more than just motivational word, it touches the reader's heart and resonates with them

Huzaifa is a voracious reader and prolific writer. He is passionate about living life to the fullest.

you can reach out to Huzaifa at

Gmail - surti.huzaifa@gmail.com

blog - www.positiveacademyhs.com

Twitter - @surtihuzi

AFTERWORD

In addition to this book, you can get a lot of related stuff on my blog www.positiveacademyhs.com

Your Free Gift

If you have received some value from this book, I'd love to have review from you on amazon.com

It will help me to reach more people and provide them with knowledge that I have gained.

Looking forward to your comments and feedback. You can send me an email at huzaifa.srt@gmail.com

I will also put-up regular content on YouTube for Positivity and Life

You can find me on YouTube at https://www.youtube.com/channel/UCETtd1RYBzqrpv9RlmoN4dA

For Positivity in your life follow me on instagram at www.instagram.com/positiveacademyhs

Dedication Page

This book is dedicated to my parents without whom I cannot become what I am today. I am grateful to my teachers, friends, grandparents, life lessons which I have learnt throughout my life.

Life is full of surprises there will be ups and downs but you need to choose your path. We always make choice life is full of choices we made and it's a journey. Choose wisely live well

Life is one time opportunity so become your greatest version by reading the books which will help you to succeed

Thank you for taking out your time and picking up this book, I am so glad that you have chosen the path to self-improvement. I am into this self-help industry for 3 years and all that I have learned is from reading the books, I am a bibliophile I love collecting books though I have not read them all but I do find the time to read book and learn every day.

1.Rich Dad Poor Dad - buy from amazon - https://amzn.to/3arC0S7

2.The Millionaire Fastlane - buy from amazon - https://amzn.to/38hWIRN

3.The Intelligent Investor - https://amzn.to/3p1aM8Y

4.Tax-Free Wealth - https://amzn.to/2Kk5ZAP

5. The 5 am club - https://amzn.to/3rbAQjO

6.Why a Students Works For C Students - https://amzn.to/37wfNQZ

7.The Richest Man in Babylon - https://amzn.to/38jltgv

8.Think & Grow Rich - https://amzn.to/3rbB1vu

9.F.U. money - https://amzn.to/2LR2UJ6

10.Experts Secret - https://amzn.to/38iwrD1

11.- 80/20 sale - https://amzn.to/3nyIwKx

12.a random walk down wall street - https://amzn.to/34qQa2h

13.against the god - https://amzn.to/2WACmh7

14.attitude is everything - https://amzn.to/34qK5D5

15.built to last -https://amzn.to/37xFmkV

16.cashflow quadrant - https://amzn.to/3akGE4y

17.Chetan bhagat three mistakes of my life - https://amzn.to/3mxr6Nj

18.real estate investing for dummies - https://amzn.to/34ruJ0O

19.common sense on mutual funds - https://amzn.to/2LRZvK7

20.copywriting dan Lok

21.crushing it garyvee - https://amzn.to/34u2teh

22.dan Lok influence 47 forbidden - https://amzn.to/2LQtUZf

23.debt free for life - https://amzn.to/3p86nBq

24.dotcom secrets - https://amzn.to/38juCWn

25.financial statement analysis - https://amzn.to/2KmGfno

26.give & take - https://amzn.to/3oYVEsW

27.goals by Brian Tracy - https://amzn.to/3mwDAoj

28.how to be a 3% man - https://amzn.to/34omXVt

29.how to buy and sell in real estate for financial freedom - https://amzn.to/2LMySWN

30.how to make money with YouTube

31.how to win friend and influence people - https://amzn.to/2LPX2jk

32.how to stop worrying and start living - https://amzn.to/37w5Ov6

33.how to think like Benjamin graham and invest like warren buffet - https://amzn.to/38myN3E

34.i will teach you to be rich -
https://amzn.to/3mz2aVq

35.real estate market valuation and analysis -
https://amzn.to/2J3UOvH

36.traders laboratory -

37.why some entrepreneurs get rich but most don't -
https://amzn.to/2J9sUOY

38.millionaire real estate agent -
https://amzn.to/34rFdO6

39.your money or your life - https://amzn.to/2WtVIEL

40.get rich live rich die rich

41.money master the game -
https://amzn.to/2KiWmCC

42.one up on wall street - https://amzn.to/37w6v7G

43.own your own corporation -
https://amzn.to/2KCk5xm

44.real estate learn to success the first time -
https://amzn.to/37xhsWE

45.rich dad prophecy - https://amzn.to/3amxNzj

46.rich dad conspiracy of the rich -
https://amzn.to/2WuPIRO

47.rich dad guide to investing -
https://amzn.to/2KimH3G

48.increase your financial IQ -
https://amzn.to/2KC2rdh

49.rich kid smart kid - https://amzn.to/2KJinKQ

50.rich dad real-life success story - https://amzn.to/3gZWbYR

Finally, you are enjoying this book so far, then I'd like to ask you for favour

Would you be kind enough to leave even just a small review for this book on amazon be clicking the relevant link below

This way it will help me to reach out to more people

51.rich dad real book of real estate - https://amzn.to/3o1iT5m

52.a second chance for your money - https://amzn.to/3nZyUbY

53.15000$ PayPal money Robert Kiyosaki

54.Millionaire Real Estate Mentor_ Investing in Real Estate_ A Comprehensive and Detailed Guide to Financial Freedom for Everyone

55.one simple idea - https://amzn.to/3nWwStq

56. Secrets of the Millionaire Mind_ Mastering the Inner Game of Wealth

57. Smart Thinking Skills

58. Stock investing for Dummies

59. stunning success

60. The $100 Start-up

61. The 4 Hours a week

62. The 7 Habits of Highly Effective People

63. The Art of Company Valuation and Financial Statement Analysis

64. The Art of Value Investing

65. The Behaviour Gap

66. The Business Of 21st Century

67. The Compound Effect

68. The Investment Answer

69. The Lean Start-up

70. The Little Book of Safe Money

71. The Mathematics of Financial Modelling and Investment Management

72. The Millionaire Next Door

73. The Millionaire Real Estate Investor

74. The Miracle Morning

75. The Monk Who Sold His Ferrari

76. The Psychology of Investing

77. The Real Estate Fast Track_ How to Create a $5,000 to $50,000 Per Month Real Estate Cash Flow

78. The Total Money Makeover

79. The Warren Buffett Way

80. The Portable MBA In Finance and Accounting

81. The Rules of Work

82. The Subtle Art of Not Giving a fu*k

83. The Midas Touch

84. the power of your subconscious mind

85. The Road to Wealth by Robert G. Allen

86. The Science of Getting Rich

87. The Side Hustle Path

88. Thinking fast and slow by Daniel Kahneman

89. Trump Strategies for Real Estate

90. The Millionaire Next Door_ The Surprising Secrets of America's Wealthy

91. Unfair Advantage_ The Power of Financial Education

92. Unshakeable Your Financial Freedom Playbook

93. Way of the Wolf_ Straight Line Selling

94. Why We Want You to Be Rich

95. you were born rich

96. Zero to One

97.Your Money or Your Life_ 9 Steps to Transforming Your Relationship with Money and Achieving Financial Independence_

98.Zero to One_ Notes on Start-ups, or How to Build the Future

99.think your way to universal wealth

100.Expert Secrets_ The Underground Playbook for Finding Your Message, building a Tribe, and Changing the World

101. Feel Alive by Ralph Smart

102. Your One Word by Evan Carmichael

103. The top 10 rules for Success by Evan Carmichael

104. You Can Heal Your Life by Louise Hay

105. Heal Your Body by Louise Hay

106. The Secret by Rhonda Byrne

107. you are a badass at making money by Jen Sincero

108. Emotional Intelligence by Daniel Goleman

109. Start with Why by Simon Sinek

110. The Power of Habit by Charles Duhigg

111. Mastery by Robert Greene

112. Outliers by Malcolm Gladwell

113. 222 Prosperity Affirmations by Justin perry

114. The game of life how to play it by Florence Scovel Shinn

115. The One thing by Gary Keller

116. The 10X Rule by Grant Cardone

117. Art of War by Sun tzu

118. Ikigai: The Japanese Secret to a Long and Happy Life

119. When I Stop Talking, You'll Know I'm Dead by Jerry Weintraub and Richard Cohen

120. Steve Jobs: The Exclusive Biography by Walter Isaacson

121. mein kampf Adolf hitler

122. The Life of Mahatma Gandhi by Louis Fischer

123. The Everything Store: Jeff Bezos and the Age of Amazon by Brad Stone

124. Elon Musk: How the Billionaire CEO of SpaceX and Tesla is Shaping our Future by Ashlee Vance

125. Man's Search for Meaning: The classic tribute to hope from the Holocaust by Viktor E Frankl

126. Autobiography of a Yogi by Paramahansa Yogananda

127. Benjamin Franklin: An American Life by Walter Isaacson

128. Einstein: His Life and Universe by Walter Isaacson

129. The Rudest Book Ever by Shwetabh Gangwar

130. Built to Serve: Find Your Purpose and Become the Leader You Were Born to Be by Evan Carmichael

131. Captivate: The Science of Succeeding with People by Vanessa Van Edwards

132. What Every Body Is Saying: An Ex-FBI Agent's Guide to Speed-Reading People by Marvin Karlins Joe Navarro

133. who moved my cheese by Spencer Johnson

134. The Secret - The Power by Rhonda Byrne

135. Influence: The Psychology of Persuasion by Cialdini B. Robert and Robert Cialdini

136. Atomic Habits: The life-changing million copy bestseller by James Clear

137. life amazing secret by gaur Gopal das

138. meditations by Marcus aurelius

139. The subtle art of not giving F**k by Mark Manson

140. the alchemist by Paulo Coelho

141. Being Mortal - Atul Gawande

142. Many Lives, Many Masters - Brian Weiss

143. Kundalini Aghora - Robert Svobod

144. The Teachings of Ramana Maharshi - Arthur Osborne

145. Three Truths of Well Being – Sadhguru

146. Think on these things - J. Krishnamurti

147. Life and Death of Krishnamurti - Lutyens Mary

148. The Conquest of Suffering - P.J. Saher

149. Zen-Yoga - P.J. Saher

150. An Introduction to Reiki - Huzaifa Surti

151. Can't Hurt Me: Master Your Mind and Defy the Odds by David Goggins

152. A New Earth: The life-changing follow up to The Power of Now. 'My No.1 guru will always be Eckhart Tolle' Chris Evans by Eckhart Tolle

153. Eat Pray Love: One Woman's Search for Everything by Elizabeth Gilbert

154. The Power of Now: A Guide to Spiritual Enlightenment by Eckhart Tolle

155. Stillness Speaks by Eckhart Tolle

156. How to win friends and influence people by Dale Carnegie

157. Sapiens: A Brief History of Humankind by Yuval Noah Harari

158. Homo Deus: A Brief History of Tomorrow by Yuval Noah Harari

159. Becoming: The No. 1 International Bestseller by Michelle Obama

160. A Promised land by Barack Obama

My Book Recommendations

Checkout my other books

BOOK OF POSITIVE AFFIRMATIONS

Powerful Success Habits to Transform Your Life: The Powerful habits that will Help you to achieve your goals and become more successful

An Introduction to Reiki

Becoming Your Greatest Version: Life Lessons to Become Your Greatest Version

Finally, you are enjoying this book so far, then I'd like to ask you for favour

Would you be kind enough to leave even just a small review for this book on amazon be clicking the relevant link below

This way it will help me to reach out to more people

Notes

☐

Notes

24

My Book Recommendations

25